Railways & Recollections 1974

Contents

Introduction	2
Out and about on Southern rails	4
Women at work	9
All change at Wimbledon	12
Freight and parcels	17
Around Reading	20
The Isle of Wight	24
London eye, 1974	26
Day trip to the South West	28
Assorted locomotives	30
North West foray	33
Railway places	37
Eastern interlude	42
Focus on diesel-hydraulics	46
1974 Happenings (1)	7
1974 Happenings (2)	43
1974 Arrivals & Departures	14
No 1 records	44
Index	48

© David Phillips 2014

Photographs © The NOSTALGIA Collection archive and David Phillips

All rights reserved. No part of this publication may be reproduced, stored in a retrieval system or transmitted, in any form or by any means, electronic, mechanical, photocopying, recording or otherwise, without prior permission in writing from Silver Link Publishing Ltd.

First published in 2014

British Library Cataloguing in Publication Data
A catalogue record for this book is available from the British Library.

ISBN 978 1 85794 403 7

Silver Link Publishing Ltd
The Trundle
Ringstead Road
Great Addington
Kettering
Northants NN14 4BW

Tel/Fax: 01536 330588
email: sales@nostalgiacollection.com
Website: www.nostalgiacollection.com

Printed and bound in the Czech Republic

Frontispiece: **ASCOT** It's June 1974 – Royal Ascot week – and the train is a special from the Midlands, hauled by Class 47 diesel No 47326. This locomotive was ordered by British Railways in 1963 and built at the Brush Falcon Works. It entered service on 25 January 1965 as D1807 and was renumbered 47326 in March 1974, three months before this photograph was taken. It started its working life in Nottingham but moved around a lot during its career, including stints at Crewe, Bristol and in South Wales. It was withdrawn in 2004 and scrapped by T. J. Thomson at Stockton on 29 October 2006.

Introduction

In the eyes of many people, the 1970s was Britain's worst decade. It was an era marked by industrial decline, political strife, terrorism and the terminal decline of a once proud nation that had formerly led the world in just about everything.

The year 1974 was typical of the decade. It started with a three-day week, imposed by Edward Heath's Conservative Government to save energy while the coal miners were on strike. In this year Heath was to take on the miners and lose – in spectacular style – when he called a General Election to let the voters decide who should run the country. The year ended with Heath's London home being bombed by the Provisional IRA.

Meanwhile the country's nationalised railways limped along. The network had been savaged by line closures in the 1960s, and the so-called modernisation that had led to the premature scrapping of the country's steam locomotives had left its wake an assortment of diesel and electric motive power – some good, some indifferent and some plain bad.

Although 6 May saw the inauguration of a full electric service on British Rail's West Coast Main Line from London Euston through to Glasgow, it was the exception.

Introduction

The rival East Coast Main Line, from London King's Cross to Edinburgh, would not be completely electrified until 1991. In fact, back in 1974 it still had another two years to wait for the InterCity 125 high-speed diesel sets to be introduced.

What little was left of the railway system of my native Norfolk was ridiculously slow. The nine-coach 'express' trains from King's Lynn to London Liverpool Street relied upon Brush Type 2 Class 31 and English Electric Type 3 Class 37 diesels, which had a theoretical top speed of 80mph but generally limped across the Fens towards Cambridge agonisingly slowly.

I knew that train only too well. I was a trainee reporter on a local newspaper, the *Wisbech Advertiser*, at that time and attended college in Harlow, Essex. It was quicker to get there by car, or motor cycle, so I made sure I passed both tests

the previous year, aged 17. For the next few years I divided my time between assorted old cars and rather nicer bikes, like the 350 Ducati Desmo I am photographed with on this page. In 1974 I was 18 and of course I didn't

think the nation had gone to the dogs. With the enthusiasm of youth, I loved the music – and even the dodgy 1970s fashions.

My boyhood love of trains had faded somewhat, due mainly to all the local branch-line closures, but also because Tivetshall Junction, where my Uncle Charlie had once ruled the roost as station master, had been among the victims of the Beeching axe. Also, the demise of steam meant that I no longer enjoyed the annual treat of a trip from London Waterloo to Southampton behind a Bulleid 'Pacific' when we went to Hampshire to see my father's family in the New Forest. But when I did stop at a level crossing in the Fens to watch a Class 31 or 37 rumble by, I'd often get out my newly-purchased Zenit B 35mm camera and capture the scene for posterity. You'll see a couple of examples of my early camera work later in this book.

But the vast majority of the images published here, of course, are from the lens of Ray Ruffell, who lived, worked and breathed railways. Ever since the 1950s he had been recording everyday scenes on Britain's ever-changing railways, and when he wasn't working on the Southern Region he would head off on holiday to other parts of the UK, where he'd inevitably take lots of snaps of the passing trains, as well as the ever-changing railway infrastructure.

Away from the trains, the biggest talking point of 1974 was 'the Troubles' of Northern Ireland, with paramilitaries from both sides of the sectarian divide committing atrocities in which innocent lives were lost.

On 1 January PM Edward Heath set up a power-sharing executive in Belfast in a bid to bring an end to the violence, but on 4 February the IRA blew up a coach on the M62 motorway in West Yorkshire, killing 12 people, including nine off-duty soldiers and two children.

On 17 May, in retaliation, the loyalist paramilitary Ulster Volunteer Force carried out bombings in Dublin and Monaghan in the Republic of Ireland in which 33 civilians died and 300 were injured. By 28 May power-sharing in the Northern Ireland Assembly had collapsed. Direct rule from Westminster followed.

On 17 June an IRA bomb exploded at the Houses of Parliament in London, damaging Westminster Hall. A month later another IRA bomb exploded in the White Tower at the Tower of London, killing one person and injuring 41. On 5 October the Guildford pub bombings killed five people, and on 21 November two pubs were bombed in central Birmingham, killing 21 people and injuring many others. On 27 November the Prevention of Terrorism Act was passed.

As mentioned earlier, on 22 December the London home of Conservative Party leader and former Prime Minister Edward Heath was bombed by the IRA. Mr Heath was out when the bomb exploded, returning just 10 minutes later.

For those who say that the England football team is a window into the state of the nation, we failed to qualify for the 1974 World Cup. And manager Alf Ramey, who had led England to victory in 1966, was sacked by the Football Association on 1 May.

Sounds gloomy, I know, but I still reckon 1974 was a good year. Read on and see what you think…

Out and about on Southern Rails

CLAPHAM If you had stood on this spot a decade earlier you would have seen a Bulleid 'Pacific' or a 'Britannia' Class steam locomotive heading this express service from London's Waterloo to Weymouth. But it is 6 July 1974 and Crompton Class 33 diesel No 33109 is hauling the nine coaches that comprise the 10.14 service to the coast. Interestingly, this locomotive has now been preserved and belongs to the Bury Diesel Group and is a regular attraction on the East Lancashire Railway. And if that's too far, you can at the time of writing even watch it in action on your computer via YouTube (type in 'diesel 33109').

Above: **SANDHURST** The hairstyle, flared trousers and rounded shirt collars of the young man on the left of the photograph confirm that this is 1974 all right! The passing train is less trendy, but a lot more interesting – it's another Crompton diesel, hauling an assortment of mail and parcels coaches on the first run of the Redhill to Crewe mail train, on 2 July. It had left Redhill at 06.05.

Right: **WINDSOR** No prizes for guessing where this photograph was taken, with HM the Queen's famous Berkshire residence on the skyline! Windsor Castle was built by William the Conqueror soon after the 1966 Norman invasion and has been occupied by a succession of monarchs since Henry I. It is said to be the Queen's favourite weekend retreat. The locomotives in the foreground are not nearly as venerable – they are Class 418 electrical multiple units (EMUs), built at Eastleigh Works near Southampton.

Above: **STAINES** A pair of gleaming Class 418 units stand in the spring sunshine on 20 May at the new EMU depot at Staines, Middlesex. It is such a hot day that the driver of the Mark III Ford Cortina – most likely the builder working on the nearby building – has left the tailgate open. The Mk III Cortina was built at Dagenham between 1970 and 1976 and this estate version was much rarer than the normal four-door saloons.

Left: **EFFINGHAM** Our photographer Ray Ruffell took this shot from the cab of the 11.14 to Waterloo via Bookham, on 13 April. The oncoming EMU is the 10.52 Guildford to Waterloo service operated by Class 423 No 7806 – one of almost 200 four-car sets built by BR at York between 1967 and 1974. This particular set was built in 1970, and many remained in service until 2005.

1974 Happenings (1)

January
- New Year's Day is celebrated as a public holiday in the UK for the first time.
- Rubik's Cube puzzle is invented by Hungarian architecture professor Erno Rubik.

February
- Fire breaks out in an office building in São Paulo, Brazil; 188 die, 282 are injured.
- Bob Latchford becomes Britain's most expensive footballer with a £350,000 transfer from Birmingham City to Everton.

March
- Turkish Airlines Flight 981 travelling from Paris to London crashes near Paris, killing all 346 aboard.
- Labour's Harold Wilson wins the UK General Election and forms a minority government.
- A Japanese Second World War soldier, Second Lieutenant Hiroo Onoda, surrenders in the Philippines, nearly 29 years after the war ended.
- Terracotta Army of Qin Shi Huang is discovered at Xi'an, China.

April
- Swedish pop group Abba win the 1974 Eurovision Song Contest with 'Waterloo'.
- Stephen King publishes his best-selling horror novel *Carrie*.
- Soviet car-maker Lada begins selling vehicles in the UK for the first time. Prices for a four-door saloon start at £999.
- Leeds United win the First Division title; Manchester United are relegated after 36 years in the top flight.

May
- Liverpool beat Newcastle United 3-0 in the FA Cup final.
- Protestant Ulster Volunteer Force explodes numerous bombs in Dublin and Monaghan, in the Republic of Ireland, killing 33 civilians and wounding almost 300.
- India successfully detonates its first nuclear bomb, becoming the sixth nation to do so. It calls it 'Project Smiling Buddha'.

June
- Explosion at a chemical plant in Flixborough, South Humberside, kills 28 people.
- A price scanner is used for the first time in a supermarket, at Troy in Ohio, USA; the first product scanned is a pack of Wrigley's chewing gum.
- Tom Baker replaces Jon Pertwee as Doctor Who.

July
- West Germany beat Holland 2–1 to win the 1974 World Cup final.
- Turkey invades Cyprus.

GUILDFORD Although only a decade old, this Class 35 'Hymek' diesel No 7028 was already an endangered species when Ray snapped it standing at Guildford station, while he was passing through on the 12.25 to Reading on 1 March. British Railways built 100 of these mixed-traffic diesels for the Western Region between 1961 and 1964, but withdrawal began in 1971 and was almost complete when this photograph was taken. The reason? The locos' non-standard hydraulic transmission. Just four survive in preservation: two on the West Somerset Railway, and one each on the Severn Valley and East Lancashire railways. Alas, No 7028 was scrapped.

Above: **READING** Here's a 'Hymek' that did survive. No 7017, pictured here on an engineer's train at Reading on 20 February, is operational on the West Somerset Railway after four years of major restoration work.

Right: **READING** Class 31 No 5695 (soon to become No 31265 under the TOPS scheme) is on an emergency ballast train at Reading. It was called into action on 20 February when contractors on nearby roadworks had caused a slip that affected the main down line.

Women at work

This page and overleaf: **EFFINGHAM** In the days of steam, engine cleaning was the dirtiest job on the railways – a tough initiation into the trade that you had to make before you could even begin to think of progression to become a fireman or, eventually, an engine driver. But times were a-changing and the advent of diesel and electric power meant that by 1974 engine cleaning was also a job for the women. Ray of course was happy to record that change at Effingham car sheds, where Peggy Tyrell (dark hair) and Rose Dixon kept the EMUs gleaming and changed the tail lamps.

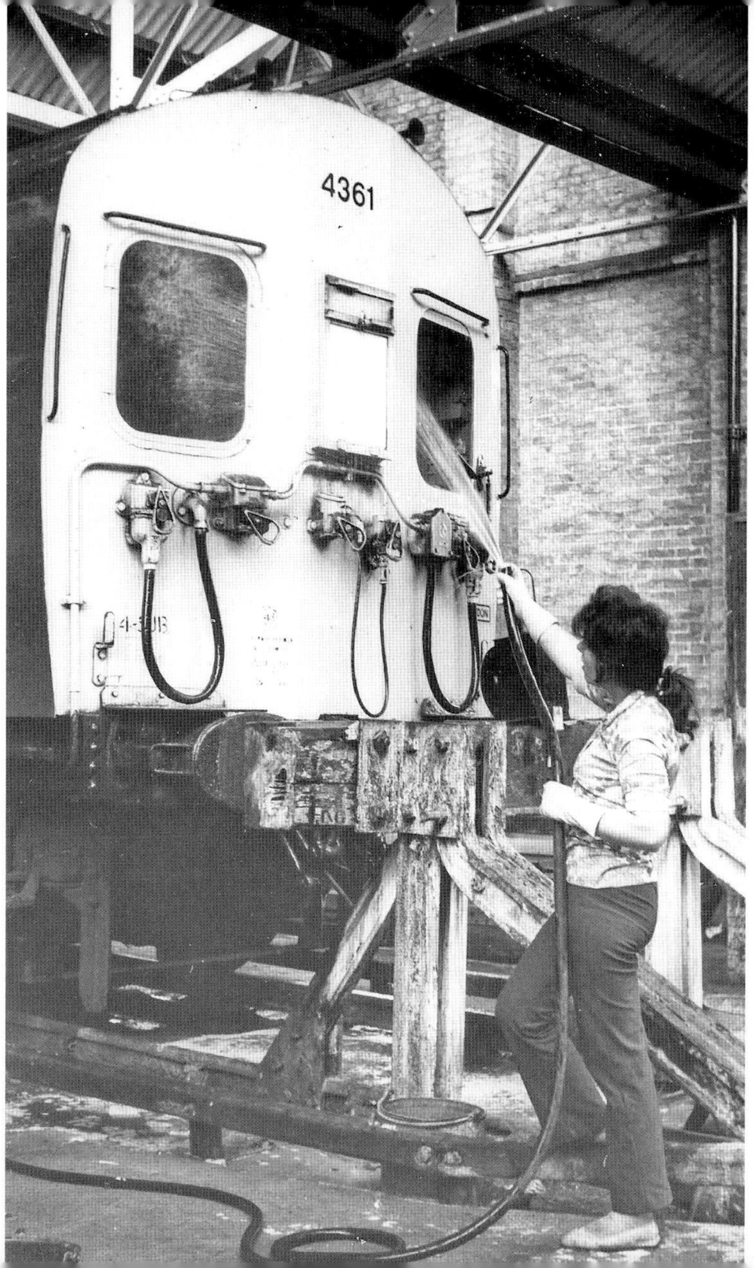

Women at work

Right and below: **READING**
Since 1967 a Railair service had operated between Reading station and Heathrow Airport. It was a popular service with railwaymen, not least because of the regular appearance on Reading's platforms of Railair hostesses in their smart uniforms. Ray took these photographs on 20 February, noting that Inspector Beckett is explaining a few points of railway procedure to hostess Mrs M. Mildenhall. Well, it certainly brought a smile to his face…

Right and below: **PLYMOUTH**
Talking of smiles, regular travellers on the Plymouth-Waterloo expresses looked forward to BR stewardess Maureen Bleser being on duty, on account of the huge grin with which she invariably greeted her customers. Looking behind the counter, we can spot plentiful supplies of bottles of Worthington E beer, together with various snacks and, bizarrely, cans of Heinz cream of tomato and mushroom soups. Presumably happy Maureen would brandish the tin opener and heat up a can on demand?

All change at Wimbledon

WIMBLEDON PARK DEPOT
Wimbledon Park Depot was a large stabling and maintenance depot located in the V of the junction of the main line to Waterloo and the line to Putney. Until the late 1950s it was also the site of the Durnsford Road power station, built by the London & South West Railway to provide power for its electrification programme.

This is the scene on 1 March, in a view of the Wimbledon Park sidings from the flyover on the line towards Clapham Junction.

Opposite top left: On the same day, this is the scene from the London end of the new suburban depot, which is being built to replace the old decrepit asbestos-clad buildings.

Opposite top right and bottom: These two views show the old sheds on the left, with the new ones under construction on the right. This was a very busy depot, where much of the suburban stock for the busy lines to the capital were stabled.

All change at Wimbledon

1974 Arrivals & Departures

Arrivals

Melanie Chisholm	Singer (Spice Girls)	12 January
Kate Moss	Model	16 January
Christian Bale	Actor	30 January
Robbie Williams	Musician	13 February
James Blunt	Singer	22 February
Matt Lucas	Comedian	5 March
Eva Mendes	Actress	5 March
Victoria Beckham	Singer and fashion designer	17 April
Penélope Cruz	Actress	28 April
Andrea Corr	Irish singer	17 May
Denise van Outen	TV presenter	27 May
Alanis Morissette	Singer	1 June
Bear Grylls	Adventurer	7 June
Hilary Swank	Actress	30 July
Emilia Fox	Actress	31 July
Brian Harvey	Singer (East 17)	8 August
Amy Adams	Actress	20 August
Tim Henman	Tennis player	6 September
Sol Campbell	Footballer	18 September
Victoria Silvstedt	Model	19 September
Keith Duffy	Singer (Boyzone)	1 October
Joaquin Phoenix	Actor	28 October
Michael Vaughan	Cricketer	29 October
Leonardo DiCaprio	Actor	November 11
Nicole Appleton	Singer (All Saints)	7 December

Departures

H. E. Bates	Novelist	(b1905)	29 January
Samuel Goldwyn	Film studio executive	(b1882)	31 January
Georges Pompidou	President of France	(b1911)	2 April
Duke Ellington	Jazz pianist and bandleader	(b1899)	24 May
Donald Crisp	Actor	(b1880)	25 May
Juan Domingo Perón	President of Argentina	(b1895)	1 July
Cass Elliott	Singer	(b1943)	29 July
Charles Lindbergh	Aviator (*Spirit of St Louis*)	(b1902)	26 August.
Ed Sullivan	US TV host	(b1901)	13 October
Eric Linklater	Author	(b1899)	7 November
Jack Benny	Comedian	(b1894)	26 December

Class 418 EMUs were commonplace here and were known as 2-SAPs (being basically 2-HAP units with 1st Class accommodation removed). They first entered service in 1957 and had a top speed of 75mph. The final slam-door EMUs were withdrawn in 2005.

Above: In the foreground of this mouth-watering line-up of EMUs in the Wimbledon sidings is a Class 421, built at York between 1970 and 1972. Most enjoyed a long service until 2005, when slam-door units were banned.

Right: Here's a real rarity that Ray spotted in the Wimbledon Park carriage sidings on 1 March. It is No 023, a former 2-HAL unit built in the 1930s. Later known as BR Class 402, the last of these were withdrawn in 1971, but this one survived as a Departmental Service Unit used by the Chief Mechanical & Electrical Engineer's stores.

Old and new side by side at the old depot on 27 April – but the new one on the left is the rarer. No 4002 was one of only two Class 445 EMUs built, as prototypes for BR's imminent second generation of EMUs. Built in 1971, they were withdrawn less than a decade later, in 1980. On the right is Departmental de-icing unit No 019.

Freight and parcels

Back in 1974 the railways were more interesting than today because of the variety of not only the locomotives but also the coaches and wagons. This was particularly the case with freight and parcels trains, which Ray photographed at every opportunity.

Above: **READING** An up parcels train arrives at Reading station on 7 March, hauled by Class 47 No 47024. A total of 512 of this class were built between 1961 and 1968. This is one of the earliest and was originally fitted with steam heating equipment; this was gradually removed or replaced through the 1970s and '80s. Those with no train heating were used for freight, while those fitted with electric heating were employed on passenger services. Although 34 of the class were saved for preservation, No 47024 was not among them.

Below: **GUILDFORD** Here's another Class 47, this time at Guildford with a stone train from Westbury heading for Gatwick on 4 March. Unfortunately No 47148 wasn't preserved, either.

Above: **READING** Coal was a hugely important fuel in 1974 as well as a hugely important source of income for British Rail. Despite the constant threat of industrial action, Britain still boasted a massive coal industry, whose workers were led by the controversial Arthur Scargill, later President of the National Union of Mineworkers; he was a thorn in the side of Prime Ministers Edward Heath, Harold Wilson, James Callaghan and, finally, Margaret Thatcher – who finally defeated him in 1984. But in the decade that preceded that confrontation, Scargill held politicians to ransom as he boosted the pay packets of his men who toiled underground. Here at Reading on 7 March is a down freight largely consisting of coal wagons and headed by a 'Western' diesel-hydraulic.

Above right: **WANDSWORTH** A Class 45 is at the head of another coal train, passing Wandsworth Town on 24 May. Ray took the photograph from the rear cab of a passing EMU.

Right: **READING** This express parcels at Reading West Junction on 20 February is heading for London, hauled by Class 31 No 31121.

Freight and parcels

Right: **READING** The shape of things to come: a down Freightliner passes Reading on 20 February. Within a few short years containerised freight like this will replace the sort of goods trains that had been a familiar sight on British railways for more than a century.

Below: **READING** ...and this is the sort of mixed freight train it would replace, photographed on the same day behind another Class 47 No 1610 at Reading.

Around Reading

Most of Ray Ruffell's working life on the railways was spent in and around Reading, but he never allowed familiarity to breed contempt – and always had a camera on hand to record the everyday events for posterity. We're so glad he did…

Right: It's 16 March, and Class 47 diesel No 47470 roars into Reading station with a down Bristol express. Partly visible in the background is the front end of another Class 47, No 47017. The Class 47 diesel-electric loco was developed by Brush Traction for BR and a total

of 512 were built at Crewe and Loughborough between 1962 and 1968. Besides being the most numerous main-line diesel on British tracks, it was – in fact still is – also immensely successful and enduring. Although most were withdrawn through the 1990s, 34 have been preserved by heritage railways and a similar number are owned by private operators, including charter companies, operating on the national network.

Left: Here's another Class 47, this time No 1932 (soon to become 47493) heading an up express near Reading West Junction on 20 February. Note the predominance of BR Mark III coaching stock (apart from the buffet car).

Above: The same location and date, but this time BR Mark II carriages are to the fore as an up West of England express roars through, headed by Class 52 No 1050 *Western Ruler*. While most of the early main-line diesels had electric transmission, the Class 52s employed hydraulic. They were commissioned by the Western Region of BR, and a total of 74 were built at Swindon and Crewe from 1961 to 1964. All were named, and the first word of the name was always 'Western'. The 'Westerns' were big, powerful, top-link locos. Legendary railway writer O. S. Nock reported a nine-coach train headed by No 1068 *Western Reliance* hitting 102mph and averaging 100mph for almost 13 miles near Slough. But the non-standard design marked them out for early withdrawal – replaced by the ubiquitous Class 47s. Although built at Crewe as recently as 1963, *Western Ruler* was scrapped just two years after this photograph was taken.

Right: Here's another Class 52, this time No 1061 *Western Envoy*, pictured at Reading on an up express on 20 February. It was scrapped in May 1975. Of the 74 Westerns built, just seven were preserved, and one – No 1023 *Western Fusilier* – is part of the National Collection at the National Railway Museum in York.

Above and left: These views of Reading Diesel Depot on the same day show the depot and sidings to be hardly a hive of activity. Perhaps it was tea break?

Opposite: These are the DMU sidings on the same day. Set L712 is a four-car Swindon 'Inter-City' unit, and is painted in BR's Intercity livery, while in the left background is a DMU in the all-blue suburban colour scheme.

The Isle of Wight

PORTSMOUTH You've no doubt heard of the busman's holiday, where the bus company worker travels by bus? Well our photographer Ray Ruffell liked nothing better than taking his wife Joan and five-year-old daughter Margaret on a true railwayman's holiday. Not only did the family travel by train, but Ray also spent much of his holiday trainspotting in new surroundings.

Here he is at Portsmouth in May 1974, on the other side of the camera as the family travels on the ferry to the Isle of Wight. For once there isn't a train in sight … but the ferry in the background belongs to Sealink, which was set up by British Rail in 1970 (hence the BR logo on the ship's funnel). Sealink remained in BR ownership until July 1984, when the Government sold it to Sea Containers for £66 million. In 1991 it was sold to Swedish operator Stena, which changed the company name to Sealink Stena Line, but the Sealink name disappeared for good in 1996 when the company was re-branded Stena Line.

The vessel in this photograph is the TSMV *Shanklin*, a passenger ferry that operated between Portsmouth and the Isle of Wight from 1951 until 1980. It was commissioned by the Southern Railway after the Second World War and built by William Denny on the Clyde. The twin-screw diesel-powered vessel replaced the coal-burning paddle steamers that had operated the route since the 19th century.

The *Shanklin* was 200 feet long with a beam of 46 feet and a draught of just 7 feet, which made it ideal for negotiating the shallow parts of the Solent. The twin Sulzer 950bhp diesel engines meant it could travel at 14.4 knots and carry up to 1,377 passengers. After its retirement from Sealink in 1980, *Shanklin* was renamed *Prince Ivanhoe* and operated as a pleasure cruiser in the Bristol Channel, but on 3 August 1981 disaster struck when she hit submerged rocks at Oxwich Point off the Gower coast of South Wales. A 60-foot gash was torn in her side and, realising she was about to sink, the ship's captain, David Neill,

The Isle of Wight

sailed her towards the shore at Horton, near Swansea, and ran her aground in shallow water. An air-sea rescue helicopter and three lifeboats came to her assistance and rescued all 450 passengers on board. Attempts to salvage the ship failed and the remains of the vessel were finally removed in 1984.

SHANKLIN For railway buffs, one of the Isle of Wight's main attractions was its trains, which since 1967 had consisted of ex-London Transport underground stock, pictured here at Shanklin station. In its heyday there were more than 50 miles of railway lines on the island, built by several companies between 1862 and 1901. Following the Grouping of 1923, they came under the control of the Southern Railway, which invested heavily in the island network and brought in new locomotives and carriages. In 1948, following nationalisation, British Railways took charge and between 1956 and 1966 several lines were closed. But the Ryde-Shanklin line, originally earmarked for closure in the Beeching Report, was electrified using the third-rail system and provided with trains that had already spent nearly 40 years working for London Underground. Electric services on the Isle of Wight commenced on 20 March 1967.

No 044, seen here, was part of London Underground's 1938 Stock, which worked mainly on the Northern and Bakerloo lines deep under the city. You can't help smiling at the thought of those subterranean workhorses enjoying retirement on the sunny Isle of Wight.

London eye 1974

Now for something completely different, as they used to say in Monty Python around the time this photograph was taken by me, in March 1974. Like Ray Ruffell, I used to take my camera most places – and on this particular day it included a climb up a chimney at County Hall, on the South Bank of the Thames, adjacent to where the London Eye now stands.

I wasn't supposed to be there. I was a journalism student at Harlow College in Essex at the time, and on this particular day my fellow trainee hack Keith Drayton and I had been getting very bored witnessing the interminable deliberations of an ILEA (Inner London Education Authority) meeting of the GLC (Greater London Council), despite the presence of a young Ken Livingstone. It was all part of our studies for our imminent public admin exam, but it was lunchtime and we were hungry, so we sneaked out of the council chamber and went looking for a canteen. Instead, on the top floor of County Hall we found an empty office with a huge open fireplace, which just happened to have a steel ladder conveniently set into its walls. We couldn't resist climbing to the top of the chimney and emerged into the grey London afternoon, with a view of the city unrivalled until the London Eye opened for business in 2000 (just a few yards from where this photograph was taken).

In the background is London's most familiar landmark, Big Ben, together with the Houses of Parliament and Westminster Abbey. In the foreground is Keith Drayton, then a trainee reporter like me, who lived in the railway town of March, Cambridgeshire, and went on to become the respected editor of the *Fenland Advertiser*. I recall that Keith and I both failed our public admin exams back at college. Serves us right.

Right: Here's a better view of Big Ben. Note how little road traffic there is crossing Westminster Bridge just after midday – and what little there is is mainly public and commercial transport. How times have changed.

London eye 1974

Left: This is the view we enjoyed of the Houses of Parliament, but of more interest in the background on the left of the photograph is Battersea Power Station, which was still belching smoke into the London sky in 1974. In fact, it continued to generate the capital's electricity until 1983. The iconic Grade II-listed structure is the biggest brick building in Europe and, at the time of writing, looks likely to be transformed into a luxury residential and commercial development (although Chelsea Football Club would apparently like to build a new stadium there).

Incidentally, although not visible on this photograph Victoria station is about half a mile away, to the left of the Houses of Parliament.

Below left: There's more smoke belching out into the capital in this photograph looking across the roofs of Waterloo station, which didn't help air quality – or visibility – on such a grey, drizzly day. But it was a much cleaner place than it had been a couple of decades earlier, when countless steam locomotives served the capital's termini.

Below right: In the background is the Post Office Tower, which at 581 feet was the tallest building in London in 1974. It remained so until 1980, when it was overtaken by the Nat West Tower. The roof of Charing Cross station is on the extreme right of this photograph.

Day trip to the South West

Above: **TAUNTON** On 6 April 1974 the Ruffell family enjoyed a day out in the South West. On the way Ray photographed this 0-4-0 tank engine belonging to the Great Western Society, under repair.

Above right: **EXETER** Here's one for DMU fans – a Class 120 unit standing at Exeter St David's. A total of 194 cars were built at Swindon Works between 1958 and 1961, and were run in three-car sets, all but nine sets going to BR's Western Region. They had a maximum speed of just 70mph. Withdrawal began in the 1980s and was complete by 1989. One set survives in preservation, on the Great Central Railway in Leicestershire.

Right: **NEWTON ABBOT** They arrived at Newton Abbot aboard the 07.30 from Paddington, hauled by Class 52 No 1010 *Western Campaigner*. This locomotive enjoyed a happier fate than most of its stablemates; built at Swindon in 1962, it was withdrawn in 1978, but instead of being scrapped was saved by the Diesel and Electric Preservation Group at the West Somerset Railway.

Day trip to the South West

Above: **NEWTON ABBOT** A view further along the platform includes two more Class 52s – Nos 1013 and 1052 – and a glimpse of a solitary Class 31, No 5655. No 1013 *Western Ranger* is another preserved locomotive and can be seen today on the Severn Valley Railway, but No 1052 *Western Viceroy* was scrapped in 1976.

Above right: **NEWTON ABBOT** The northbound Devonian arrives, hauled by Class 45 No 45010. A total of 127 of these powerful locos were built at BR's Derby and Crewe works between 1960 and 1962, and operated on the Midland Main Line from London St Pancras to Nottingham, Derby and Sheffield. Withdrawn from service in March 1985, No 45010 was scrapped in Glasgow in 1988. Known as the 'Peaks', 11 of these engines survive in preservation.

Right: **DAWLISH** Shortly before the Ruffells' day trip, the South West had been lashed by storms, as was to happen again disastrously 40 years later in 2014. Ray recorded this damage at Dawlish from the window of the 15.55 train from Paignton.

Assorted locomotives

Left: **READING** The 15.55 from Paignton brought the family back to Reading, where Joan and little Margaret chat to the driver of Class 52 No 1022 *Western Sentinel*, which was built at Swindon in 1963 and scrapped in 1978.

Below left: **READING** Earlier, at Guildford, we met Class 35 No 7028, which was soon to be scrapped. Here at Reading on 20 February is one of its siblings, No 7017, which survived into preservation. This particular 'Hymek' was built by Beyer Peacock at Manchester in 1962 and initially allocated to Bristol Bath Road. It was withdrawn in March 1975 and lives on with the Diesel and Electric Preservation Society.

Below: **READING** This 0-6-0 Ruston diesel shunter was captured outside Reading engine sheds in all its grimy glory. No PWM (Permanent Way Machine) 653 was one of five built specifically for Departmental use in 1959, and later became Class 97 No 97653. It was only scrapped in 2011.

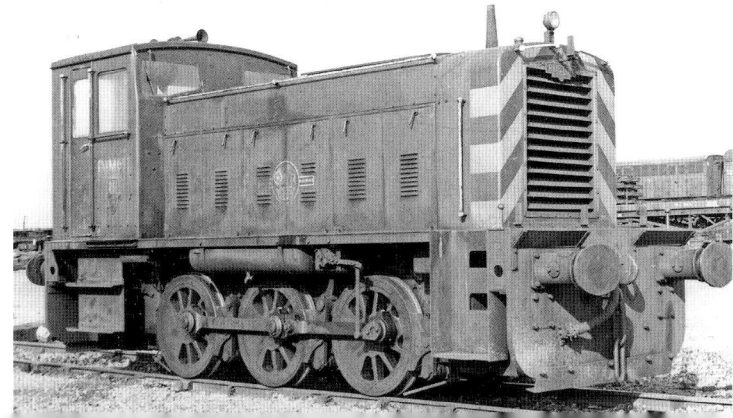

Assorted locomotives

Above: **READING** This 0-4-0 Fowler shunter belonged to the Gas Board.

Above right: **TOLWORTH** By 1974 the railway preservation movement was already saving retired BR diesels from the cutter's torch. Class 04 shunter No D2310 was already looking good when Ray photographed it in private use at Tolworth Coal Concentration Depot at Tolworth. It is now a popular attraction on the heritage Battlefield Line, one of 19 Class 04s saved for preservation. A total of 148 of these locos were built between 1948 and 1962. They had a top speed of 25mph and were rated at just over 200bhp, but much more importantly they boasted 15,650lb/ft of torque.

Right: **READING** Although most common on the Eastern Region, quite a few Class 31 locomotives found their way to the Western Region, including No 31254, photographed at Reading in February. Some 263 of these locos were built by Brush Traction between 1957 and 1962.

READING Here's one of the most distinctive – some would say the most handsome – diesel locomotives ever to run on our rails. BR's Type 4 'Warship' Class 42 locos numbered just 38. They were built between 1958 and 1961 at Swindon under licence from the German Federal Railway (they were a scaled-down version of the Germans' successful V200 design). This is No 821, named *Greyhound*, which was withdrawn in December 1972 but had already been preserved when Ray photographed it on 7 March 1974.

North West foray

Most years Ray took his wife Joan and daughter Margaret for a summer holiday in the North West. July 1974 was no exception and the Ruffell family duly set off – by train of course – from London Euston on the West Coast Main Line, which by now was electrified throughout.

EUSTON This was the scene on the morning of 20 July. On the left is Class 87 No 87024 ready to head to Glasgow and beyond with the 09.35 'Clansman', while on the right is No 86252 at the head of the 09.40 for Aberystwyth. Ray clearly had time to kill – the Ruffell family would be taking the 10.15 for Blackpool.

At the time this photograph was taken, No 87024 had been in service for just three months. In 1978 it would be named *Lord of the Isles* and continue in service until 2004, when it was withdrawn. It was scrapped a year later. A total of 36 Class 87 electric locomotives were built by BR Engineering between 1973 and 1975 to work passenger trains on the West Coast Main Line. They transferred to Virgin Trains on privatisation and continued in service until replaced by the new 'Pendolino' tilting trains.

Left: **LEYLAND** Ray took this photograph from his train as it passed the Leyland Motor Works at Leyland, Lancashire. The diminutive locomotive is a Planet diesel, an industrial loco manufactured by F. C. Hibberd of Park Royal, London.

Below: **PRESTON** Another photograph from the moving train, this time of a Class 86 heading south near Preston, Lancashire. The Class 86 was British Rail's 'standard' electric loco of the 1960s; 100 were built between 1965 and 1968 to replace steam traction on the West Coast Main Line, and were used to haul passenger and freight trains. Most remained in service until the early 2000s.

Right: **LANCASTER** No Ruffell holiday would be complete without a trainspotting session for Ray. On 23 July he chose Lancaster station, where he photographed this pair of two-car DMUs. On the left is the 09.22 service about to depart for Morecambe, while alongside is the 09.19 for Carlisle via Barrow.

Below: **LANCASTER** The 08.01 Carlisle-Euston express pulls into Lancaster headed by Class 86 86024.

Left: **LANCASTER** Another Class 86 is hauling a southbound Freightliner with the assistance of Class 85 No E3074. Class 85 comprised 40 locomotives built between 1961 to 1964, which were essentially prototypes for evaluation by BR, and precursors of the later Class 86. Most were scrapped in the 1989-91, including No E3074, which faced the cutter's torch in 1989.

Below left: **LANCASTER** Here's another of the Class 86 precursors, this time Class 81 No E3005, which was one of 25 built between 1959 and 1964. They were designed by British Thomson-Houston, although before work was completed the company had amalgamated with Metropolitan Vickers to form Associated Electrical Industries, and it was under that name that the locos were built under subcontract by Birmingham Railway Carriage & Wagon, in Smethwick. No E3005 entered service in 1960 and was withdrawn in 1990. On 23 July 1974 it is seen hauling an express from Crewe to Carlisle.

Railway places

Of course, Ray Ruffell's evocative photographs are not just of locomotives and rolling stock – they are also about the people and places associated with Britain's railways. With infrastructure dating back to the first half of the 19th century, there was certainly plenty of interest.

Right: **FLEET** A typical scene in Hampshire Commuterland as passengers await the arrival of the 08.06 from Basingstoke. Within an hour they could all be at their desks in London.

Below: **FLEET** Why did British Rail try to make its stations look like glorified Portakabins in the 1960s? This ugly monstrosity is what greeted passengers at Fleet in 1974.

READING That's better – the ornate Victoriana at Reading General is appropriate for such an important station. Classic car enthusiasts will be able to spot a Morris Marina, a Vauxhall Viva, a Ford Escort van and Ford Cortina Mks I, II and III, among others.

Left: **WOKING** In 1885 Canon Allen Edwards, supported by the workers of the London & South Western Railway, opened an orphanage in Clapham, London, for the children of railwaymen. In 1909 it moved to a 9-acre site in Woking, with a £24,000 budget to provide a home for 150 fatherless children. Following the Grouping of 1923 it was opened up to children from across the Southern Railway. The building of a hospital block in 1930 was followed by a new accommodation wing in 1935 housing a further 90 children. During the Second World War the whole site was commandeered for a hospital, reverting back to an orphanage in 1946. It was renamed the Southern Railwaymen's Home for Children in the 1960s.

Below: **READING** Biscuit lovers will be interested to know that this is the entrance to a tunnel that once served private sidings for Huntley & Palmer at Reading. By 1974 it was disused, but Ray noted that it had three ventilation shafts.

Right: **LITTLE SANDHURST** The paternal side of the railway industry of old is illustrated here by 'Uncle' Ernie Fisher, the popular ex-cable and track manager who had started his railway career on the Southern Railway. Now, in retirement, he was allowed to stay on in his beloved railway cottage at Little Sandhurst. Note the lovingly tended vegetable garden.

Below: **WATERLOO** We're about to leave the Southern Region, but before we do we'll pay a final visit to the place where so many journeys begin and end – London Waterloo. Here Class 33 33109 is about to depart with the 10.14 express to Weymouth, on 6 July.

WATERLOO This is the bustling scene inside Waterloo on 2 March 1974. The scale of the grand terminus can be appreciated from Ray's vantage point, opposite Platform 1.

Eastern Interlude

Ray Ruffell seldom ventured onto Eastern Region rails. If he had made the trip into East Anglia – former Great Eastern country – he'd have found a lot of Class 37 and Class 31 diesels, along with a bewildering assortment of DMUs. This was the first part of the country to lose its steam engines, and as a result received large numbers of the earliest diesels. The branch lines were awash with DMUs including Derby Lightweights, Cravens and Metro-Cammells.

By 1974, however, the infamous Beeching axe had been responsible for the closure of most of the branch lines in this neck of the woods and most of the rarities had disappeared. My local main line – King's Lynn to Cambridge via Ely – was traversed mainly by the aforementioned 37s and 31s.

MAGDALEN ROAD In its haste to destroy what was left of West Norfolk's rail facilities, BR even closed this popular station on the main line. Situated between the villages of Watlington and Magdalen, it was a lifeline for locals, who kicked up a stink when it closed in 1969. Eventually it reopened in 1974, a year after I took this photograph.

In 1989 the station was renamed Watlington, probably because the village of that name had by then grown into a sizeable commuting community. It also happened to have been the original name of the station when it opened in 1862. And if you're a fan of obscure railway literature, this is the station when Arthur Randell, author of *Fenland Railwayman*, started his career. The book recounts his days on former Great Eastern metals, particularly his time at Waldersea signal box on the former Wisbech-March line. When passenger services on that line ceased following the Beeching axe, he became a professional mole-catcher and wrote a second book – you've guessed it – *Fenland Mole Catcher*.

The careworn Class 31 here is hauling a nine-coach train from London Liverpool Street and will be arriving in King's Lynn in about 10 minutes. These days, the London terminus for King's Lynn trains is King's Cross.

Incidentally, although the station is now known as Watlington, the sign on the signal box adjacent to the crossing still says 'Magdalen Road'.

Eastern interlude

STOW About 3 miles south of Magdalen Road is Stow crossing, situated close to the Great Ouse Relief Channel, a massive artificial drainage channel 11 miles long, 100 yards wide and 13 feet deep, excavated in the wake of the tragic 1947 floods.

Rumbling by the crossing gates on a spring evening in 1974 is a mineral train headed by a Class 37 locomotive. The wagons are carrying high-quality sand excavated from British Industrial Sand's quarries between Leziate and Middleton, in West Norfolk. It was for this purpose that a short stretch of the former King's Lynn-East Dereham line was kept open by BR after the rest of the line was axed in the late 1960s.

The Class 37 locos were known by railway enthusiasts as 'Tractors' on account of the agricultural sound s emanating from the diesel engine, which drove the electric traction motors. They had a top speed of 90mph.

1974 Happenings (2)

August
- US President Richard Nixon announces his resignation following the Watergate scandal, and is succeeded by Vice President Gerald Ford.
- An express train bound for Germany from Belgrade derails in Zagreb, Yugoslavia (now Croatia), killing more than 150 passengers.

September
- TWA Flight 841 crashes into the sea shortly after take-off from Athens, after a bomb explodes in the hold, killing 88 people.
- Ceefax is started by the BBC.

October
- The Labour Government of Harold Wilson wins the second General Election of the year, with a slender three-seat majority.
- The 'Rumble in the Jungle' takes place in Kinshasa, Zaire, where Muhammad Ali knocks out George Foreman in eight rounds to regain the heavyweight boxing title.
- McDonald's opens its first UK restaurant in Woolwich, London.

November
- In Birmingham, two pubs are bombed by the IRA, killing 21 people.
- Lord Lucan disappears after the murder of his children's nanny.

December
- A Boeing 727 crashes near Dulles Airport during a storm, killing all 92 people on board.
- The Australian city of Darwin is almost completely destroyed by Cyclone Tracy.
- On 30th Japanese soldier Teruo Nakamura surrenders on the Indonesian island of Morota, 34 years after beginning service in the Second World War.
- Former government minister John Stonehouse is arrested in Australia after faking his own death.

1974 No 1 Records

January
Merry Xmas Everybody — Slade
You Won't Find Another Fool Like Me — New Seekers
Tiger Feet — Mud

February
Devil Gate Drive — Suzi Quatro

March
Jealous Mind — Alvin Stardust
Billy Don't Be a Hero — Paper Lace

April
Seasons in the Sun — Terry Jacks

May
Waterloo — Abba
Sugar Baby Love — Rubettes

June
The Streak — Ray Stevens
Always Yours — Gary Glitter
She — Charles Aznavour

July
Rock Your Baby — George McCrae

August
When Will I See You Again — Three Degrees
Love Me for a Reason — Osmonds

September
Kung Fu Fighting — Carl Douglas

October
Annie's Song — John Denver
Sad Sweet Dreamer — Sweet Sensation
Everything I Own — Ken Boothe

November
Gonna Make You A Star — David Essex

December
You're The First, The Last, My Everything — Barry White
Lonely This Christmas — Mud

Right: **READING** Powering away from Reading on 20 February, the 13.10 departure (1B35) for the West of England is in the capable hands of Class 52 No D1013 *Western Ranger*. Built at Swindon some 12 years earlier, D1013 was to be withdrawn on 28 February 1977, having hauled the 'Western Tribute' rail tour (Paddington-Swindon-Swansea-Bristol-Plymouth-Newbury-Paddington) two days earlier in the company of No D1023 *Western Fusilier*. Both locos have been preserved, D1013 by the Western Locomotive Association and D1023 as part of the National Collection.

Focus on diesel-hydraulics

Above: **READING** Later on 20 February Ray captured another West of England express but unfortunately the locomotive number was not recorded, perhaps a record exists somewhere of the loco hauling 1B:45 that day?

PAIGNTON At the other end of the West of England service on 6 April, awaiting the dropping of the starting signal, is Class 52 No D1022 *Western Sentinel*. Sadly this loco did not survive the cutter's torch, being scrapped in December 1978 at Swindon Works, also its birthplace in 1963.

Focus on diesel-hydraulics

Right: **READING** Following the demise of steam on British Railways during the period 1965-1968 the D prefix denoting Diesel and the E prefix denoting Electric were deemed unnecessary and were gradually phased out. In 1974 it was common to see the numbers still prefixed by a D but not 'picked out' as seen here on Class 35 'Hymek' No (D)7017 resting between duties on 20 February. This loco survives in preservation.

Below: **SANDHURST** Sister loco No (D)7016 is seen running light engine back to Oxford from Redhill having earlier passed through with the 21.39 Bradford to Redhill 'parcels' working on 25 July. Sadly graffiti has already become commonplace on the rail network with the waiting shelter having been given the treatment!

Index

General
Bleser, Maureen 11
Buffet services 11
Carriage cleaning 9-10
Dixon, Rose 9-10
Fisher, Ernie 40
Huntley & Palmer private sidings, Reading 39
Leyland Motor Works shunter 34
Mildenhall, Mrs M. 11
'Railair' service 11
Sealink 24
Shanklin, TSMV 24
Tyrell, Peggy 9-10

Locations
Ascot 1
Clapham 4
County Hall, London, view from 26-27
Dawlish 29
Effingham 6, 9-10
Euston 33
Exeter 28
Fleet 37
Guildford 7, 17, 48
Lancaster 35-36
Leyland 34
Magdalen Road 42
Newton Abbot 28-29
Paignton 46
Plymouth 11
Portsmouth 24
Preston 34
Reading 8, 11, 17, 18, 19, 20-23, 30, 31, 32, 45, 47; diesel depot 22-23; station buildings 38
Sandhurst 5, 47
Shanklin 25
Staines 6
Stow (Norfolk) 43
Taunton 28
Tolworth 31
Wandsworth 18
Waterloo 40-41
Wimbledon Park depot 12-16
Windsor 5
Woking, children's home 39

Locomotives
Diesel-electric
Class 04 31
Class 31 8, 18, 31, 42
Class 33 4, 5, 40
Class 42 'Warship' 32
Class 45 18, 29
Class 47 1, 17, 19, 20
Class 97 departmental shunter 30

Diesel-hydraulic
Class 35 'Hymek' 7, 8, 30, 47, 48
Class 52 'Western' 18, 21, 28, 29, 30, 45, 46

Electric
Class 86 34, 35-36
Class 87 33

Multiple units
Diesel 35
Class 120 28
'Inter-City' 23

Electric 12-13
2-HAL 15
Class 418 5, 6, 14
Class 421 15
Class 423 6
Class 445 16
De-icing unit 16
Isle of Wight 25

GUILDFORD The 21.39 'parcels' from Bradford features again in this shot captured on 28 June passing through Guildford en route to Redhill. The diesel-hydraulic in charge on this run is Class 35 'Hymek' No (D)7029.

Acknowledgements

Many thanks to the family of the late Ray Ruffell, without whose efforts to photograph and record the changing railway scene in 1974 this book would not have been possible.